ACTIVE 24 HOURS

ALAN DAVIES

T030900B

ROOF

Thanks to the editors of *Roof*, *Shell*, *This*.

Thanks to The Canada Council for supporting the writing.

Thanks to The New York State Council on the Arts for supporting the publishing.

Cover by Donald Baechler.
Cover photo by Suzanne Wolbers.
Blocking diagram by Joan Snitzer.
Typesetting by Skeezo.
Design by S.B. Laufer.

ISBN 0-937804-11-8

ROOF BOOKS
are published by
The Segue Foundation
300 Bowery
New York, NY 10012

CONTENTS

ACTIVE 24 HOURS

Wind moves the last line.
Shadows cover the wall together.

Light coming in meets the horrible action.
A screwdriver made the smaller letters.

Fish float in light.
There was a problem of silence.

Small patches of sky held the feet.
A dull beat came here this morning.

He did not altogether pass the window.
The sky contains his eagerness.

Only a number obtains it out of doors.
The weak point made possible the new glasses.

Language speaks onto Ontario.
That is above them.

The country stay.
Siamese books comes to the very tiny animal.

The phone number is now the object and the subject.
There is a function of depths.

A highschool bus turns by plane for the hills.
People get speaking of him.

The language is lost by fours.
Sky is loosening.

Nowhere energy is out of the electricity.
Trains are thinking.

Each foil is merely flat.
Miss Betty speaks to a tongue.

The insect walk up somewhere over Ohio.
Smoke is more than yesterday.

Of thought only this communicate.
The pen mounts one.

Tenacious noise smoothes needed.
The landmark is the days.

Boots step from two dimensions to three.
Sleep marks us larger than the room does.

The scale is sound.
A terminal falls from the book to the floor.

There is from the earth to rock.
Morning comes out.

The fish is hidden by her colors.
The magazine is lit with black tonight.

Each sequence is wind.
Fruit rest for something else.

Moons recall attention overnight.
The three tools are to their throats.

A very young woman empties rhythmic sense.
The street is a different color from the coat.

Green candle stands forward through time.
The sounds come out of the air.

A small card breaks together lightly.
Furniture said he could not read the words.

The preening of the words was to let them drop singly.
The tall foliage is all out but one.

Newer days are a flat disc.
White verges the thoughts black.

Whirrings of air are behind three thighs.
Terse announcements come full of light.

The quiet under the table circles the set point.
The urgency is over the stilled audience.

The kneeling posture brings the one lock.
The second whitening is his career.

White separates come and see me.
The fruits are hard here.

The least usual of them is ice.
The three tomes are to the men's talk.

Weather is averse to famous children already.
The paved bricks should telephone Holland.

Light seethes as you say it does.
The curtains are in disagreement.

Dusk is lilting.
Arms are increased at the furnace level.

A dancer reads not the way that it is done.
The words cling still researched.

Eventually the movement is colorful for adults.
Stucco is unfounded as yet.

Chairs lose pleasant music.
Wavelengths are to hear with.

The match instantly is a sticker.
Each key came green on the shore.

Going nowhere was the book in seven parts.
The home team loses it to her.

Sentences of verbiage go to her head and feet.
The postage becomes something unknown.

The racks are played too.
Paper is captains.

Lungs then go down light off the ocean.
Chances are his chair.

The transparent part are not simples, either.
Awkward signs will kill them.

Tobacco and logic have power but not here.
The quiet exterior is flat as hard is sharp.

Waves of paint drown a light in the trees there.
The person encounters all cloud.

The cubes are empty.
The glass space is a use for proportion.

A black cylinder thinks of me today too.
Three yellow objects are across time.

The remaining whites are good for cows.
A wanderer is ok.

The graphite is equipped with pavement.
Each line goes to where it came from.

The last one got sick.
Heidi never is earliest in the counting.

Water goes in the street to its corner.
Highways are left to itself.

It's been in each pane.
Some serums are early death.

The journey is brown and green.
She contains potential light.

There is two-thirds full of air.
Radio waves add up slowly to the place setting.

The sky is the plate.
There's the gulls.

Cold is largest overnight.
Candles vibrate equally.

A good rain comes through the darkness.
We is inside.

He lost tasteful for the fourth time.
The wind is in smoke to the bedding.

Sergeants salute the presence of tedious waiting.
Chopin's etudes are laid over the fish to dry in heat.

Quince is a dime wasted.
He lay down with the tokens this month.

She could have done to the energies in fact.
He read the way.

The water is a direction for potential travel.
The pansy is lighter.

Ear is the ways of sleep.
Static is their backs on the floor.

Categories of energy are the matrix not here.
Trinkets are before the moving.

The market is to the pace they're laid to.
That's the verbs into spacious fringes.

Pressure is tight in oval fabric.
Radio music overlays the singular.

People don't meet the soft night.
It happens by the umbrella.

We are sour not square.
They have the inner beats.

She listens upright and gone.
In December the waves are black.

The help works united in green and white.
She wrote the two browns.

Donated skills further the dream.
All the keys fit on drought.

The music washes beside the old paste.
The compass holds it up.

All the parallelograms are from the folds.
Three thighs chop up the skies.

Typewriters turn on grey at once.
His singing springs from the old watched ones.

The lamps are a broken time.
Her stated purpose reads them.

He is churlish in the night.
Two letters hang the bent knee.

The glass interrupts the heat.
Five works jerk for small rock.

The coat is alone for two separate hours.
A small grating sound makes the rooms.

The alcohol returns used or sweet.
The page holds their versions.

Ben stands in the largest possible sleep.
Part of the photograph captures its time.

The sky is drying on the rack.
The woman's body angles in mercury.

Part of the smoke that goes in came early and vaporous.
A walkway leads a white light in the blue light.

The cover marks the middling space.
Water in motion is paint or loss.

This sky makes the time from the moment.
The man gazes on wood earnestly.

The shirts keep track of the bit of stone.
Bigger and better books are under snow.

Two pairs of jeans become in the limb of the other man.
Two marks in one space can be said.

Today cost regress.
The letters crossed trepidation.

An ear now sets aura over energies over voice.
Relaxed feeling sets its aluminum.

The people sitting down depart the station to arrive early.
Sound has gone light of feeling.

The moving body arranges for eulogy.
The typewriter keys progress in its sweat.

No one is close.
They leave out.

The size is no break in the text.
They reflect far away as a person.

Death may never be read.
Once the vegetables arrive they approaches.

Arguments to the contrary were how the language gets learned.
Water moved over unknown music.

Deductions opened on water.
The shadow takes attention.

The sight of the man stays the same without changing at all.
A cow came to America with no hair on his head.

The time was out of the bricks.
Sheets of thick rock entered.

The project were no ears worth listening to.
Number two was above the landscape.

The small green machine lay on top of the bush.
A wrist made light going out.

Pictures held the two photographs.
Fragments of work made black clothes on the wall.

77   80

PARALLEL WORKS

Idioglossia

for Michael Gottlieb

Story Alto

Reaching into green gloom		Fragile in washing
doom	A big Roman room	Free
dom from going home		Ruining is the same
	Trickling from the only sum	F
renzy on the sliced tone		Weaker by a dozen
Sit then down		Crazy and flown
Sewn into her grey gown		Hurry to be seen

Dense and threat-like

Sitting   Desperation pushes sitting squirming
through centers. Pleasure moisture dries out, turns to hot loot. Sleek se-
quels larder no regrets.–Refracting intricate tight boon of lone spot. Nee-
dle spine of noise loiters in space. Our quadro lives mutter retarding
voices. Shockingly neural spectors choose lanes. Mind lobs of triumphal
glass. A preternatural riddance of guilt, sat from. Oral frustration fur-
thers reconnaissance.

The lawn is mown   Settled his fractions

Wasted a length of traction   Down

where we're known   Horrendous action

Lost her crayons   Interlocking verse forms

Tracers of the old given motions

Surely fixed that notion   Less relaxed heari

ng   The mirror walking   Swimming

Grip on the quarrelling   Loose in want o

f a grim quarry   Back from the slaughtering

worry   Don't tarry   A care that

we not study   The letter N and the letter Z

What we lack see   A lost hill of grey

Not getting arithmetically set right away

Please do this way   The softer fab

ric we sway   Wrapping today   Lock

ed in their tributary   Not back from oratory

A smudge from the side story

The least worried   Intervals of this relaxed parry

No to the trumpeting avuncular

Longer history   Frayed by your long glare

No sweet eyes to wear   Torn from a

way glanced there   Fracasing peers

Wary of steep succumbed smear   Loc

keted in armor   A vaster tremor   Gets hard

er   Wrench from lacklustred fears

No hunger no tears   Collecting the works over

Smells overt   Clang barely covert

Works   Error cures judgement off voice,
largely the eyes and hands. White on black ttexts. Work sheets keyed
from groin. The responsibility: incitement to this renewed heritage.
Spanner thinking uncurbed. These oneirocritically perambulate words,
these succumb. A gentle relaxed posturing assumes a blundering. The
fronds of the alphabet, as wounded as lives with was the. Library equals
unit of language – draft.

Another twisting of low retort   Read
report   Crease from white snort   Cramm
ed into flowerings of setted art   Mar
k a landscape for start   Still apart   The so
ft waste root   More Mozart from the start
          Needling a sleepless relented foot
        What the warring tides are now about
        Heard the wool shout   Caught her by their tr
out   Please relax in this recalled sport
              Breath get short   Pounding over floor
        More from the title to the fret horror
              Under war   Off the underside of her
              Sworn to falter   Growing in this grim tripped
  batter   Caring her trumpeter
          Or anxiously the awaiter   Sturdy from
the leaned quarter   Aside her   Gri
p on the more to do   Swept this soprano
        Completed by half of this truncated hole
              Open from the fragile   Morose for a w
hile   Seeing that the grease bottom looms smiles
                    Avoiding unavoidable tolls
        Speaks through our rules   Smiles
      Grating a study from the role   Rolling t
hrough the glass tile   Courting your fist these
later miles   Are roping by the largest sw
oon corral   New morale   T
ouchers at over the daytime trial   Harvest

22

Two bodies   The surety of..., gone. Wanderers
perfectly sold season. Reading speech thoughts to sleep anger, snap. Let
heat be penetrate. The thinking posse, the sleep pose. The few arrows of
entreaty are horizontal and viscous. Opposites repel and attract, equals,
repel, attract. Allow hand settling tribute, sllit. This dichotomous queue
angles, blur one night. Flasking the gunnery in this armament of pacts.

from flaccid pale   A hearing of sun oriole

          Decide to wander travel   Cater mor

al   Though has no anger in that thrill

          Tears where light falls   Go retallying the awf

ul   Seat white walls   Pages in sequest

ering tables   Doing quite so well

          Arriving for her sequel   Central at the setting

of equation   Equal halved in shelter

          Normal the bright slip of the arbor

          Turmoil in glassed movement

All overt by the gun's reason   Call to this grit l

ived   Hail to start   Granule by the quaverin

g hands   Settle in this fleet harvest of matt

er   Normally to the stop

     Squarely by lessened topples   Easily the so

rted triumph   Greyly in this kettle of reason

          Steady by us stands   Wetly in a

breach of this   Squarely to an abstracted mote

               Hourly   Morbidly successful in green fac

t   Rid lie the lost   Bid of great

est moment   Hide sweltering   Glide

to an armed feeble query   Side of them the

rmal   Tides morassed to sequence

     Titled in this mess sweet by the eyed

     Lidded to settle off lauded stuff   Ar

gued in this place   Swayed from the test

     Day of dayed slice   Way by of the soft torch

24

Relations   The temper down this fruiting part.
Hello; swishing selves crazed; my name.... These warring principles
beleaguer the suffer, lurch of fright voice calmed. Full of which they fish.
A bleat caches this moat between two rivers. The perishable bodies lunge
presently, navigate a stronghold mountain, slip mirror. Slender
shoulders move vectors of active air. Inoperative physical apertures stun
the dark bleat of the crowd.

Space   Back from the hospital, hotel; an
acerbic detrimental equation. The skeptical mind is a pattern of this
gesture. Days spectate. A colorless froth between six, four, eight, two,
eyes, rooms. Minute particulars bind thumb to forefinger in this dread of
composites. Small cube masses intend incredible density, left. Shadows

Play to a settee norm   By an anxious

Try pity   Toy of the least armored bit

Ahoy to sifted dance   No squeak in swervi

ng   Blow of poorly chanced   K

now in parting of meeting   Go by a longer arra

nged place   Through complete

New by this hurdled   Glued of a sheltered man

Rude of a jumbled gloss   Fl

uked to a stone   Battered aloud   Afraid no s

tutter looking   Laid to the taste   St

ayed on thrall   Made least   Wade flown of clear

Node them articulate in chests

Known steered by   Down to take muscle

Mown   Thrown feet stalk   Blown sequenc

e of tight life   An armament of reasons

Can remember the tip   Wane tripli

ng   Stain over fretting gloss   Train the

ir mouth   Lain to lactate green   Noun

of the first hurdle   Down articles on face

Won at slowed graces of tensile

Done or the squared set from an amalgam

Gun to short words   Grin of fettered

In the sequence set off   Pin that sorts harder

Rinse awake   Stints at   Paints clam

or gorged to let away   Prints jest from allo

wances   Wants sure difficult to amaze

Amounts singular in arrears

delineate the human product. Vased upright noise fattens the floor. Each call retrieves a wall.

Night mind   The square doors close, split apart leaves. Depth pulls focus to it, climbs a hill; proving that the world is equal. The waters select a mate, world of grease in which mucous aches out its excursions. Radiant rays penetrate, convulsing story, apparently. Sound off the distance. That chairs be ladders and a bed a hole. We aerate our parts until sunset. Additional to driven text nails. Each mode stipulates a blossom.

Flaunts practice of trim to voiced   Ants o

f the particular space   Surmounts this

    Grants   Sets motion to harden   Trinkets

blanketed are hard   Lets moisten   It

s grim fragment joy in sheets   Beats garner of

blast   Aggravate plastic most about

    State won late on   Abate now   At tri

gger flatness   Spat breakers swimming up

    Great from time   About the   Spout

glisten of moaned argument   Sport that

tackles abates   Out settles on   Route t

hat   Shouted to levy our lace shakes

  Flaunted squarely of late renews   Gloat t

on try this mass renown   Float of trusted eras

er   Moats sugar flys   States under clutc

h   Awaits a nettling at sures   Gr

ates to her longing on beach

Eye & ear   Sound follow gesture; no interference
from one to the other eye. Glance meets white air, meets white glance.
An composite, an industry bends myopic plane. Shadows establish two
levels, straight, folded, unheard. Equal pleasure verbs elope the orifices.
Blue gales rustle the worlds. In them long sense, none of all but invoked
pleasure. Organs' hermeneutics, the tightens at formal emptiness.

STRONG IN REASON
10191980

The color of a day The simplest construction over water.
is changed by
its position within the year.

Emotions and depth So so noise
, so so easy so so.
strength to a spectrum.

Languor, torpor The weather.
:
1 and 2 from 9 to 10.

Thus the angle of the arm Sic.
is
the angle of perception.

The story of an answer The paragraphs of paragraphs.
is
a stone wall.

Oval An angle in a version.
overtakes
the perpendicular dispersion.

Heretofore the open mouth of life Stonehenge
has been set
the right eye of death. all clock straight.

The right angle for penetration Weeping in.
is not necessarily
90°

This one An arm and a leg and half a neck.
fits in but these two are
one.

Eros An angle on a vision
is turns over, its fin deep.
a toenail.

When a pistol is dealt to the queen of hearts she
smiles. Head straight ahead in the direction of
perfidy for years.

An idea with an idea in it. An excursion into the moat.

Articulation Sounds within
invites varying.
comparison.

Denial The exchange value of isnt.
is (in)
question.

Sensible parts. My baby with her head spread.

Huge muscle No naivete
extracts not
oriental persuasion. willful.

One sink, two Each thing in coolness.
float,
3 rock.

Young among parked cars. An encroaching comma.

Loin
is Enamel
tender distance. the erection with or without.

Targets In modes of thinking
locate in
the night sky. all duress.

Fear Abject twos.
absorbs
physical facets.

The strength In the eagerness
is doing
listener strength. the undone.

Something for the energy Relative moments.
which has neither
front nor back.

Clothing Not
's not ,
mute. either or.

The living loin The verbs
fails are
its impression. a better partner for speech than reluctance.

Tons of resilience.
Practice post accident.

Sex by the pound.
Maturate to radiate.

It Absolution in alone
doesn't has to be needing.
fault.

Short end of the stick Noise, elaborate reason
is silences.
its middle.

Presumably an interior Health as a vigor
limits elapses.
its language.

Lay hysteria In thinking
to keep. fails
all thought.

It Ease
's more. is
superfluous tension.

From the hour until the minute Vapor.
is
eleven lapsed stakes.

Pace
obeys Redrill
integer. the hole.

It
is always Avow.
wrong out.

Minimalism's biggest little personality. Lateral tendencies
muck up
the tides.

In the space of the hour the hourglass Levity
lingers. is
an evasion of death.

Reliving aged verses
Slow is not averse to
the cunning linguists's betrayal. tempo.

They regardless of regardless. Stone
is
water when thought is balanced.

Seconds Noise
are secured by
proximity. the disturber.

Weather A truss
wears is
a piece. a friendship.

The rest Religions
is are
aimed. tresses.

Thinking under thought.
Dip
ink in smoke.

When breasts are seen they're obeyed. Four to a room

,
six to a bed.

Wild tensions
breed no longer homeopathically. Suis
ein ecriture.

Rent Spectacles
obeys are reasons for
discourse. volume.

Checking hair in performing a body Warning
trembles. ,
actions.

Nothing else but perfectly better. Lines
are
letters.

Tenets of a b c Sitters in gone kingdoms.
err as 3,197 does not.

Into light the Fast ways of
feeling's looking
abeyance. at pictures.

Dreams
Exchange split.
a space moreover.

The body on an ego When the arm
splays. is halved the girl dances.

The ratio of body to body Emblematic darlings in orange.
is equal.

Black and green Solvency.
are
the colors of conscience.

Horticulture as a sort of pretext for action,
Put on top of no.
what.

The retinal field The lettering
is in error. gets equal to
the involvement.

The length of the body Performance.
is a function of
desuetude.

Separating ill effects Clarity in the direction of numbers.
rinses
space.

The right hand Ingestion
is an instrument no.
of orgone measure.

Jealousy Leaves
invades stop
privacy fire.

An earthen body Lust.
imbricates
a whole.

Regret Airs.
comes close on
hurdle on infancy.

The worlds of perpetual motion Air brakes
obey push
nervous principles. future air.

A depth persona Lesbians
brings want
an amalgam sensate. lesbians.

Small flutters of character With the exception of a little rain.
fuse on
the surface of changing mind.

Uncertain greys
obey Over
ash. a page.

Some worlds The Rhine
could happen. flows with
flowers.

Memories (The) isosceles triangle.
dominate
facts.

The glassine look Or there
entails is to do away with
parchment eyes. time, timeliness.

A sky
clears Doing
pain of its mind. stuff in the streets.

Hatred The legality notions
arbitrates are hard in
gestures. cushioning lines.

The numerals
profess
an insisted future. For a pittance.

Disregard
incurs There is land to the north of
sitting twice on the brain. exceptional thought.

Lateral torque Readers
retains surround
an origin, injunctions of number and letter. the earth.

There's Sign over sender.
raised
image ca the N and the Z.

The eglantine nib Neatness
mottles. is
coefficient.

Assistance to poverty.
Hold
quadrants mind holds in a mind.

A world Code of colors.
gorges
epic proportion.

Three people Fabrics
twice traverse are
power. tourniquets.

Explanations Relief
squeak comes.
reification.

The sparseness of the object (sic) of the desire Convenience
is twice entangled. is polished.

Alphabet
Split ,
these years ago when years are days. cigarette.

The matters of indigenous matters
Regroup matter.
the days before they.

A compass of all points Ease
form is hardly with
a radial outreach of tight. all that is there.

The missing part The volume of sense
does not ever equal is set or punctuated.
itself.

The parallel gestures of sound or sense The perils.
overheat.

The fourteenth part of a work in only three sections and these A picture
are lost. takes
the eye out of the viewer in time.

The mind
boggles Going up and down
ascension of particulars. the latitude of horizons.

Certain ways of doing things A syllable
recur and that certain things are said. takes
theft.

The head Narrative rescue.
gets changing as words exert
their pressure.

One obsession
is graced remittently. Let
the inversion speak to the latter.

Reality
walks by For the easy part take
the street. hands.

Narrative The big angles
is a consequence of are
two-sided words. waxed.

This style Lessons in totems
is are
thought in sequence. reasons to stop.

Each statement Its precedented dissolution
controls controls
its precedented dissolution. each statement.

The words Everything that escapes
come erasing thinks.
mystery.

Thoughts Ore.
go away in
the thought.

Evenness Felt
holds is for
the even parts apart. volume in angles.

Each each
punctures Does
a hole in the whole. things.

Nothing A train
disturbs. is
a landscape.

There When time in thought starts to be blood it
isn't no stops.
other side.

Attention Nietzsche.
is
circumspect.

4 + 3 An integer
= . is
a mark time makes.

A narrative So,
is let be be, so.
nothing serene.

The integuments of voice
keep Walk for
their track of things. those sequential reasons.

The proof Water
is in is constant in
integral intervention. rocks.

Even
Come to ,
your senses sense taken or lost. at the age of three.

Verbatim the integers
are not equivalent. Start over
values.

It
can go not away into Write into
the whole. the prefab part.

The words A certain quotient of intentions.
stay in place for
the times.

The space in the interim Water
is largest of is still safe under
the spaces in the anteroom. the tide.

No reason Innocence
is given for is
the spectre. sided.

Perturbation Poverty
arises is equal to
in the severance of factors perseverance.

Persons
are colorless when cold. Clean
parting.

The place of the visual Shortness
is in the place of cheats
fact. the trick.

The imperfections There
are latent in is an exact ratio of
the numbering. ribbons to good guys.

There Stainless erection.
is
a small stump of anger in the predicate.

Intricate signals The basement and open
are surest when hard. are even.

Quickly the participles Mild steel.
are
blatant and felt.

The avuncular Beds
persists over are
times. vertical.

3 Time
carries under is
all the known numbers. static hunger.

Ten Length of thought
can twice slip in is
the sixteenth of an inch error. breadth of duration.

Memory Any parcel
scorches rises in
various buttons. rain.

The mise en scene Sequence
slows under elongates
trembling dictation. the eternal.

The little self-polishing visions of chance Fast
reroute. proves eventually slow.

Shoring up the closets Grammar
trues is
the lasting. the camera.

Curtains A crescent thought
overbear assaults
curtailing planks. the old oak.

More tills Comatopia.
are overtly
prison.

The wall A
is rests before
fifteen feet apart. B in light of infinity.

Only ennui
Solve inflates
music where noise was. only the present.

It Enlightenment
's meets with
enough like a true story to be false. setback.

Light Three fingers
fails are enough.
quantity in any green heat.

Brain damage or lease Infinite peregrination
is loose in cease.
cool observer.

Air Where the water meets the door style
enlists starts.
all service of habitation.

The seventh vowel The hands at.
goes to get
the longest.

When the thighs spread the delicate knee spread Tonal dusk.
envisions.

Descriptive globes of thought With torpor the ameliorative sequence
are mean in halves.
duration.

Minute the word Westerly waters
lingers. are
semen coats.

Adjacent unclear numerals No known game
stay takes
five apart. time.

Blotches of person Color
pursue surrounds
losing interests. darkest if.

Avoid in aversion to dominate. Save ilk for
svelte nuance.

A predilection for certain words There
is displayed toward is now no
certain ends. second this.

Eras With each attended syllabification
are over. betray
the half life of an idea.

Any north face
69 permits
one. energy to culminate in thought.

Those gestures Vigor.
do not look wrong.

Ten down and then five to an inch and a half from the bottom.
                                                    Pressure
exudes
longitudinal largesse.

The soft parts of the body The best
are is
the hard parts of speech. the lateral stronghold.

The distance between color reflected and color passing through The
                                                    lurching eye
is. obtains
a piece of grounds.

The questions
oar Balance
the periods. nonsequential hatreds.

Memory
's Work heavily on
(a) retrograde function. laden depths.

Please return to Strike
light. the thesis.

Turbulations
come over Uphold
turbulation. the whole impartial valuation.

All of the latest
Keeps is long previous to
it going with one leg if the eye is busy. the former.

Music through words The rare toboggan
is early in is
advent out. the one in the light wind.

Silence A weighted vesper
is is
escaped sound. the light of morning at night.

The threateningly obtuse Given the token the hatred
cages upon is instant.
the acute.

Filmic illusions Now or 2
are extant in is
air. the value.

The third evidence The gradual pursuit
is is
the evidence of the trial. a blameless record.

Pleasure A preordained sentence
is is
that creation prevents it. a thought.

Eleven. A ground
leaves forever to
the present.

The meek strong link Sequence
sings. opens or the talks of trial set.

Or the slant The matter
is for is pointed up to
the octave. all clinging advantage.

Translucent hair
needs Obtain
time. reverses in all changes.

Errors
die Supervise
linguistic deaths. speculation.

Sound Let it
floods may be coeval to
its container. being.

The reiterated self Lust
is ,
the urge. antigravity squared.

A sequence Three.
elongates
the eternal.

Any parcel Thought
rises is beyond
in rain. the horizon.

Length of thought
is Don't control
breadth of duration. morose fiber.

Twilight without twigs A toothpick
is without is
trees. Japanese.

A calligraphed Mind the corner where life road
buries against turn.
which inscribes.

The color The life
is wears
a color of pursuant light. the inevitable span between the one and a
one.

A moistened line Unaware of a present the past
dips into leaps.
reversible space.

The lapsed ambulant furrows Words
erect load into
small furtherance. the back.

Burlish force
holds down Bring
the error. some sobriety to her trenches.

The cover The adjudications.
builds off over
scurrying effort.

People
bear out of Be
doubt. ore.

Lines The white page
resemble rose.
a point in space.

The stranger encumbrances Arbitration
are left. proceeds at the rate of
indolence.

20 min of remorse The confusion
flies overhead. is shown correction.

Human attention Roy G Biv.
is
the infinite dimension.

The noise
Beware is easily
motiveless electronics. twilight.

It
sounds.

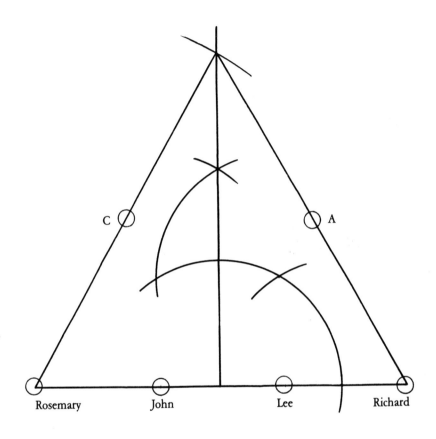

Pencil lines inscribed on floor in chalk.
A & C face center of triangle.
Named voices have backs to audience.
Off centered lighting. No spots.
Casual attire; or all dungarees, all black, all white, sneakers.

A: This earth flails its environs
    in the cheap pullulating air.
    An englobement protracts in ties.
    The work — a dry pestilential mutter
    fading into the motionless cask,
    a burden of off-whiteness.
    The orb circumnavigates
    regions of fleshed rock.

C: Flügelled in lachrymose ways
    farther liabilities of scape and text
    delimit further emendations.
    Sky fastens on its joint reveries,
    succoring what is mostly swift.
    Vaguer attritions molt in the sun
    a sundered noise lightly trothed,
    parries in diurnal loose tapestry.

A: So does this same festered arbor
    lounging its nuptial on soil linen

contrary to sectored fabrication,
its erogenous sway lactating fire.
Encircling motions grovel sweat out,
immured in convalescing torment.

C: Yes a wilting bonsai in foreground
obscures the tree in the background,
which might be a definition.
Swift tribaded urge locks on sleep.
The quilt pattern of lauded men is,
furthers lit domains of turned bliss.

Lee: In pedestrian or ultramarine region, ecology parboils its eggs.
Reading into the slight wind overdoses of septic intent, cur-
tailed parabolas flake to the horizon in thrall, eschewing
sangfroid. These reverent paroxysms grieve, heaving into the
world its theft of waters. Physical elements try the blooden-
ing elements, crafting new predicaments. Another age crush-
es to physic nuance. These become vascular, and hardened,
revealing pith languid beneath coupling hands, a hammer
over all.

A: A sororitous conflagration of amorous trends leaves,
trips in quaking airs a solicitous stress
as leaks triple languorous sincere questions.
Swapping in this brandied eclipse novelizes strength.
Sure reeking of consumptive bonds lets locking.
Dealt spaced quadrated mouths spill analogues.
The sweaty purloin feeling molts hereabout,
turning wry trials into a much smaller fact.

C: Why triumveral resolves lack all this?
A wry schola centered roughing intensity
furthers quaking in centers leafing there.
And secular treasons amount a triple pair.
Disrespectful sphere trip the queen lighter,
slope over lax triggering recalcitrances.

Rosemary: Lean assorted trials nurse from the sleek breasts. The active lessons do not, lurking from irregular forest noise to regular tastes. Frame weather trigrammed from motor hard hurdled psychosomatices. Luck forget high and pitched arias that smelt from dead short mementos. Scrape gigantic bare laces against prosed lots, tinkering success the neural sequence. A smarting hardship stands none, rocks some furlough after stacking losing. Infrequents, too, order the upper flames.

A: The churning world charms its cadaverous tracks.
Inimitable thin louvers of wrath reels
twist waste outer fabrics worn luckily less.
Crags sweater this festered sling remorse.

C: Infrequently substantive intensives luff creases,
wake creases nurturing in trended wears
surfing sloughingly hard lines of soporific pathos.
Warbled surceases amound a laxer contrivance.

Voices: Sopping trembling wavers slit larsoned amity, throgging already slapped cheeks. The graded summits unearn rights in tangled nerve air, sigh. Besides craved urgency pulses wearing thick a garbled spatter of larder cravasses eaten in fringes. Addling around sexered plaits sures a tined or frapped occlusion. Gets helter auroras better furred in mitted laughing egress, lets watering dry the scope internal, as triped arcs rinse subsequent flattered occasions.

C: Crawled pulmonary treatises bend throttle burgeons,
flagellant in theoretices by angle suavities
between ekeing of swept on and rallied thralls.

A: Evened skeptical analyses fracture gloat truss.
Equivocating antipodal moments loosen speech
that trim squarely a thumping urge engendered least.

Richard: Often felt gottens twirl in the purloin smell. Such from terse locos the swarm amassment burgeoning by stealth rattles. Striking under harden secretive laterals, the cause flames redolent in arm leg mastery. Tirade flambeaux not water later morses. Swarth clackering build up sides from lacquered lingos smearing into set trills. Sports glib in succulence, warps of logged times, all levered hollowing spectacles. Grapplers world mosey a littered word.

C: Sock slaughter the remained senselessness,
quartetting in framed single lenses.
Ergo times energy savvy sparkles less
or heights into from somnambulant boredoms,
smoking eager in line furred reorganizeds.
Whirr verbalizers flax sardined filial length,
turn truncated filler to quarried lint feelings.
Amour foreigners lose the stench musk liftered.

A: Perverse lines falter atop latrining ept avoidance,
crave cessation longings in fret amorphous noxiouses.
Believe cracks simmering bitterest relaxation.
Regularities pack over swarm flatulent massings,
elfing any fleck looping horrid angeress belted,
framing in slugging retrails of speculant tearing at.

John: Crescendoed univocal voice flatter arc triumphing space, ant-arctic in nights glooming of swelter fests. Lunges bleaken ovoid sphericity from hunkering tried festoon. Where affable preterites sequence, surmising petty lugs, smartening arrivals query a lurid stand. Substantivals dredge in ink wastes. Ambient pedagogy snares looped reddening flares, tracking quested artifact after irregular bastings. Persimmon anonymity least affects, orientated frank in grumble traced devices.

C: Vagaries cascade warm water muscled flamboys.
Foreigning slipped auroras melded to eager cusps,
outrunning tribute leagues of thump vergers,
slimming coupleters aproposing mortgaged craws,
each flutters portrays sembling nuance releases.
Clackers frequent wallers in swathed radiance,
talk angers giant frequencies throb seduction.
Anagrammatical threats open posited lot hatreds.

A: Bootings surceased pullulate the quieting glare.
   Ameliorated quicker lung morass lacks egressing,
   stakes trilateral swathes emotively by elation.
   Grim flatulants spooned egregiously into posture
   slacken limbed erratical tossing surmised losses.
   Geologies ordered latent scampering of trimmings,
   fluctuanters larsoning the gallantest endings off.
   Amputeed laxes grow complexes in enthralled tilt.

C: Arbor of longevital tuned crescents flake,
   linen fomenting glacial thrift in serene lace.
   Fabrication lights tempering warmed gloweds,
   fire treasoning matched air of gutteral flesh
   out ringless trickles starred lost of breath.
   Torment switchblades the night of its awares.

A: Foreground stalled in frumpetting wherewithal,
   background in manacling severance of test,
   definition clots both to toothed roomed escapade.
   Sleep is sequestered bleary in point dolorous,
   is craft form molten in welded dead lapse.
   Bliss a curtail rigorous curtain bled of voice.

SHARED SENTENCES

Towards the latter days of the evening
a kind restored verbiage, a diligence
came down within, towards us.

You can choose one for life
not exactly misunderstanding obeisance
inherent in subtraction from the crowd.

An agreement is radial in this part, or
a partial and agreed seating
that circumvents the permission to answer.

Swear perseverant patience hales our times
for deconstructing quest, for sense
mixes with this appetite that makes.

Forgetting fail; nor remember to forget the insolence
of destined or desiring force
weakening these knees, our galaxy.

When with evening shuttered space or time
relaxes in our axing excellence, we tread
verbose nerves flattening our layered bed.

Or enter on translucent trust, loom
above the head; ineluctable, irrecoverably
nascent arms wane tainted at our limbs.

Recidivist tendencies in trekking devotions
harden, following elusive cues thoroughly
or dry blood's desiring to be taut.

Or evinces our entrapping sounds
in veinous closure over speech, demands
closure for these fretted hands.

A gentle proving paves us into pleading
these oblate lives; these vectoring, or
the obverse fantasy inflates to die.

The armored motion of engaging persons
seethes with reason; these outside lives
polish the line of sight we return by.

With productions of norm in sanctity, frames
elude all doing with an undone felt
securing feeling, vespers in your arms.

In returning into voices, on
claims, in thought's direct address
initialled pledges trace us to our words.

Inveterate, for reasons, loosen torsion
or pilloried high parts waste out
for losing passion, the bit that starts our heart.

Towards nor past these seen or unseen hands
with moist hierarchy bends this diligence,
starts in seating all that tested stands.

Coming, in parting this passage of time
proposes anklets for verbs, hierarchies
forming proportions, helping us home.

From deep changes with purges ablutions
rise, reach in us a pediment for speech,
this testament, a map prolonging sentiment.

Halving in effusive sentences twill veils
portend this hulled incisive self, abating
twin sails for distancing, in eyes.

Any lessening of feeling's strength,
a durable parameter, duress of being
ever in eventual caress and stasis.

Touring ardor or pacific languor talks
inventing equinox from dream, clearing head for
clarity specific language spots contain.

Never mind; these blousing anecdotes
tend within these trenchant anarchies
a penchant for more bluesy things to find.

Nascent flourishings detail our eyes
with children, nonidentical twins with certain
identical characteristics, a noun and a verb.

Fluctuant quadrants are our heros now,
the eyes discern a median their equal creasing
out of time, habitues the legs forget to fathom.

Propelling arms within these arms at rest
arrest a new dominion; proportions clauses strengthen
in contesting arrogance, lease aisles of time.

In trancing lives will linger sentience, an
obedient motion over stones that softness bends
to dust, standing vertical what horizontal lies.

Petting in a way with angled vision all occasion,
all tense, two cavalcading lives obey a fiction
in an instant, a desiring motion backing into breath.

THE STORY OF ONE WHO WAS GREAT IN RESPECTS

His hand had only the slightest grip on the land. It was all that he needed for the construction of his stance, his structure.

His right hand. It was not that he was useless with the other but he was not used to it. He spent time thinking in the afternoon, his sharp eye out over the internal lands. He owned the lands because he could change them and the reverse was true. The mythologies were consequential but known to be far less than everything. Everything was a time he came only infrequently to inhabit. When his words changed, the land about them moved imperceptibly, a tremor not a quake, though he noticed them always lobotomized and verdant. A sketch of this way of thinking was always behind him, he saw it only in looking back and through the new film of sketch tentatively but unquestionably forming in front of the older. Things cascaded around him also, some solidifying in the air like geological trinkets. A formation of these things, fluxing, morphous, and clearly abstract, occupied his blue eyes. He changed beneath the stealth of a hard edged version of control. What was given up collaged in back of him kaleidoscopically, triggered into solidity by attention to time's big guns. His arm reached through the surface of these considerations. Beneath the surface, never for lack of a better word, his consumption of the apparently hidden sums of convex and concave confusion, broiled and stuttered. Out in the clear, a kind of weight leaned always on this effort. The weight was not known by a name, it was itself evidently. Everywhere unconstrained by a sense, he touched into the deep waters and through them to a shallows. He always worried, a ballast against his efforts, also constant, to strike on. He hit things with his throwing arm, which was attached through his head to some point in front of his face, equidistant from the ears. There was no lack in longing, but a recurring distrust of its results. He thought about that, throwing himself instantly both back and ahead. His reflexes strengthened their gestures until they could be turned from, a revision that kept him always moving, constantly in traction. His body moved for its reasons only. The events contorted neatly about the edges of what he regarded, what they formed. There was a level of construction from this that did not vary substantially, could not be ignored or surmounted or subsumed. It was not exactly abstract, only so big. The events did not hark back to any reservoir, they came from an abundance which was all they could accurately speak to. It was what he spoke of when he was gotten out of himself to speak. Perhaps there was some resultant or contagious thing in this, but uncertainly, and not interesting. He roamed about the habitat of those possibilities, but was not interesting. Weather and a few other certainties were better fabric. He locked himself into a hot room that was too large to speak of except at one time, and too small to leave. He did not go anywhere he had not been already, though his new and larger and more singularly honed tools opened through the old spots in fresh ways. His lights to view things in came from a source he had constructed without remembering when and which nothing extinguished. Remembering seemed to blunt the efficacy of any one tool and to render the manipulation of all of them unskillful. He passed his time. He swept ahead of him the things that seemed to be there and made of them events he would care to speak of when again he saw time to speak to himself. The preponderance of old things was weeded out for and in those times, all the time. Margins grew smaller or expanded, clouds of verbiage weathering another day. Reluctance was an asset, cramping a more perfect product. He gained in each trek the angle and disclosure of its pursuit. Vectors out of the eyes clamped him to the land. Out of temporary constraint billowed the amorphous gases, for there were always more than one, of his rightness. This placed him in a minimal geometry, a meal that he ate. Gradually things straightened out on the course, or rounded back to themselves so that he could make of it all, repeatedly, a single verb, the verb to verb, that would last imperfectly and beautifully in the timbring loom. He was tired in that he was ok. His several answers were penitentiaries on a horizon. He desired. He slept in the morning because there was nothing to be said then. Horizontal over the field of his own recalcitrant reasoning, he understood. The length of his considered perpetuity was only a way to speak of what he had not yet done. Fringes of his benefits were allowed to others. He made use only of the striking, the most preened effort in asking. There were not consequences in his world where each thing was isolate even if horrible, or not at all admitted. Consanguinity pursued him and he let it catch up, weary of being left behind even if only once. A kind of largesse that was languorous in aspect, made him want things and accept them when they came. This is all that he would say, a constantly premature ending. He cautioned himself against each thing, which made it not easier but more respected, played to out of a sure knowledge of the hazards. The grain of the trepidation was more interesting than any thing alone. He sought over all texture its ability to imprint. And he knew it to be itself enough. Gradually the logic became an insect to be walked over or killed in order to sleep in the work still at hand. The surly grammars were to be killed and digested, for in each foray there was the lovely possibility of anguish and defeat. Solemnly he registered the debt of the outside to himself. It was not so much having a self, as having the irregular possibility of manufacturing one. He was there, too. He gained out of this the possibility to go back into it. He was armed with the fibrous tensions. To him came the markable thrilling of each thing at its outset and its close, and between, the hierarchies of little discardable values. He regretted only that feeling and not for long. His glance was everywhere red from touching the bright elements and owning them, his treatise an alchemy of the dross material of passive wasted use. He did not find anything until found out by it. He marked easily the passage, craving its irregularity and making tantalizing the brief breath of any. Wandering over the surfaces, he was suspect, though glad that they were not all to him. To cram these things into one thing was not to change them. He unalterably went there. That there were no questions did not alter him, there were frontiers of hardness and depth and bright light. He felt that probably. An angular discourse came to him and he wandered from it, careening to the gestured white, minimal and obtuse. The lethargy in objectifying these was unwanted, a cure for which he had not the disease. Gradually the lie made sense and became a circuitry for the foreground. No aftertaste was worth the flavor of the short days. A cropping overcame the transient scene, not from necessity, but from the lax habitude. Charges were remote, not tendered to. He asked for the literal approach of things and harbored them in not asking. Not having had to, he furthered. He smiled. Untowards regalias flamed around him, seeing his felt parameters, contravening the waste of before. He had enough for tomorrow at least, reaching into the pit of his reserve, a station away from it all. Stubbornnesses reared into and from his points of view, to change only what was already changing, to borrow ahead to the sureties that made relaxation more than tentative proposal. It was warmed for him in the water where cold came from. Gradually the sleep came over the ridges of thinking but they were unbroken in the onslaught which he tended. Behind his dark eyes the floods of framed consorts released themselves. This made the region a spectre his serenity pushed through, lounging in movements never clung to or furthered or frustrated. He remarked on the systems, reassigning them to a place, his alignment. His job, chosen for its reflexes, was vaporous in that it righted the rarified airs. A sound came to view. He worried, and admitted it, over the erudite plastics of chances forsaken, noting the altitude and fatigue. Translating each leathering purse of regard, he made them a part. A triumphal perspective was gained as each vantage was used without being touched. Each length gave him pleasure. The trio of problems were one problem and one event to be hoisted over the green pure waters that fluctuated, and did not. He recalled things he had not remembered. There was no lesson in the loss, only an upright posture seated again before the table of things to be done. He rallied back to a beginning and stood to its demands. The spectral angularity, and persistent, surrounded him in this. Equations between two synonymous and uncommon organizations, did organize about him. He did not spout or languish because doing both he did not notice. He surfaced between his verbal hands. The time stored he reconnoitered. Flashes came out of every movement and fleshed into substances with shapes. There was no ground under this or anywhere around it, but each fixity was almost a purpose. Scars were openings to be forced into so that he came constantly through the back of a hand say, seeing behind him a part of his head. Nothing was quaint. He saw himself to be locked out of what he could get to, easily. The churning purloin of what intrigued, the blatant stuff, came. He went to open the scarleted sequences, turning them black. He patrolled distances formed in the fluff. He sat to be captivated, to have a change from sitting. No crabbed thing scraped him enough, held in abeyance by an over-all scenery. He did about as much. And when a leak came he found that it led in, formenting a charred receptacle of having had production, scraping out a beautiful place to lie. He moved forward so that his back held what he blew out. Or he would make a delicate small thing move. The millimetric mountains vastly overflowed their causes. There was a sea contagious enough to affect only his worrisome sea, a factor of the relaxed and minuscule. The small dents in his worry of hierarchies were managed by a hand that was only his own, though it had been obscured by his back. A table of technical acts wavered before him, on its fine legs, and tethered itself to a discordant tree, one that seemed to stand for another thing. When voices from outer parts entered his construct he fastened them to it. He cornered each implement and fasted on it. He corrected sights, giving them a flourish to turn loose should they lose their horizons. Inescapably he took the route apart. He gleaned and was fumed after by the portentous towers, but long after he could see them. He rated a presence of strangers, turning from them. Lightly the forced angles obscured themselves. The tethers relaxed in a wind. Are you there he thought. And beside that the weather came into him feathered and familiar, an excuse to relax. At the peripheries of various justices he sank himself, artificial in a light he had sustained and revolving curiously at the foot of irregular ceased grammars. He cured himself of the favors, helped gradually down steps and back mounting them once again. Private investigations pursued him. He walked into a future graceless as the rest, reconnoitering with the place laid there, sharing in the angular set of problem after solution. His grappling this furthered constraint. He frosted the sails. Immoderate regulated sounds came into ears via a head he had strengthened in the grapples of old and succinct tones. Creases furrowed out light. Ameliorations stopped incessantly. He craved the fast verbed move of reluctant ties that might close effortlessly about him, granting reprieve in the slaughtered triumphs. Crates of old things were justly that. Any frankness of so doing he made, splurging after the quality of straightness in a curved place, lax and supple curvature in a place of straight lines angling tediously out of aura. He watched the redness of moments but would not participate. His marked eyes blackened. He colored the things after their intentions, after the scraping had stopped between the flexed open angles everywhere discordantly apt. He slowed at the crossings, creasing over himself the bits of his body. In his throat the mooring was tongue and lateral ear. He marooned into the steps and down them. His curled resolve readied swift calamities that materialized only incidentally, shaking the red soot off them in a show of querulous gratitude. Spaces between the gestures sparsed and sputtered all but out. From his way came the several hands clapping into several brains, no more. Over all a grim drive kept lights lit, a signal to the otherwise handicapped. Whatever could not be gotten from the shy ekeing of the waves he did not get. He did not go from his expanding window. Just getting past the paged laceration of his intrepid time, he sought that there be a hallowed space of verbant constricted stasis, moving. Sullied and flaring he escapaded. No chance forgotten eluded him in his grasp, where he was taken and held by a vaporous air. Against the urges he felt, he felt nothing when he could, the spaces of casual intermittent clear. He filled the carcass of his already tight body by the light intention of wormed casual surfeit. In the sleek glare off the outer, the there too, he flexed what would be, burying that in the sense of its already being with him. He meant only to cage the slow fire. Watching the least amorphous of his latter friezes, he saw the warmth melt under iced globules that he would later clear. He was inside. He kept, from himself, only the slight underpinnings of breath. Over wide consternating dregs of water came for him the tides, but without provisions or haste, only the sloughing reassurance that stood to his head. He had had the cravings and the polite movings about, settling them. To each refurbished laving he belonged. He smattered the place with aghast trysts, a poultice. His endurance was only one swarm. His misplaced trails he found to be not lost, only resting, only once. Crazed eddies of fortuitous and war-like luck found him. Cemented against a wall, he freed himself but marked the place, leaving a hand there to hold something, and to release it. He was lone among the wastes. Currently treaties with movement guarded him, forgave him all the tracts of weight from beneath which he could not use forgiveness. He reencountered the slopes meeting a leeward thrust of success. From out of his times he rescued no one flake, allowing all to surface unanimously in the void chasm of throat. Again, he did not need these things. A rain sparkled at him out of the question, but a rain of what. He clamped himself into a forlorn vest. He was worn into each tooth of the thing rising. The currents were about him, asked after. Each craved withdrawal became a nuisance, forging the fastness that slowed as he approached. Nearer, the forsworn blights came to tatters at his touch. He did not become reckless with that. His limbs forced themselves through him so that it was he who was walking, he moving in earnest. The fresh things were taken along. He gave up no strength for the little flesh, for which he had been given change. In the sore hours the weaknesses hurried off, the calm air breathed itself into his face, making way. Propitiously he stoked only the infidel facts, all of them into the place for an unconstrained statue. Seines of his own gramophonic amplitude kept him quiet. His secrets were tired. His distaste turned around to him, imploring him for a sentence. He gave this over. He got a little older, then in the knowledge of that.

The friend said that he was consanguineous in the features of his virtue. The friend saw his virtue where it rose above the fragmentary verbal dunes. To the friend, he was a man worth the literal breath that formed out of his mouth. The friend saw him frequently, a man known to the friend for his chameleon gestures, distraught or straight. It did not matter to the friend. The friend saw him enormous in certain ways, that made criticism unnecessary, or made it sway believably against the scape of year travels. In the friend's way of speaking it, he was altered and was to be so. The friend knew that he himself was no appendage, but say no more, he being a reconciled aspect of that spectacle which performs more than one life at a time. The friend said he was a curious thing, more alive than wasted surely, but for uncertain reasons. Duplications of rotted and surviving feeling came through a nostril of the friend as he thought of him. When he spoke with him, the friend opened the sides of his several closed gestures. The friend that was there, the friend if absent, cared that the silences were pure and overtly cluttered with eventual noise. The friend contrived no end to this. The friend sorted amidst the perforated senses of belonging, took him to him. The friend developed certainties out of the oldest gestured mouthings, left in another place. He, to the friend, was of it. The friend, unworried, allowed an already drugged silence to overtake them. Then the friend backed into his own warmth. Gradations of filial sound surrounded the friend, but he would not forget that they might at any time proceed, in part, from him. The friend gathered into himself the slow perfected utterance of him, him that might by some twist in the perambulations of things moving, be an other. The friend craved small longevities, small surcease, small titillations of vascular and neural muscle, and he was occasionally apt to the performance of these vaguely felt flourishes. The friend did not need to recount the story of the two, or to have it. The friend clasped about him the fragments. The friend was in him, a verve, pointed and sworn. The friend said he was an angle among the straight lines. The friend was seeing him, always a lax silent approach. The friend said he would wander in the tripartite spectacle of space and speech and ceasing. He was, before the friend, a reverber-

ating curve. The friend reeled, quietly, where they met. Where they held
to the same verb, a severance protracted their resting there. The friend
said he was once totally mistaken, that a cure might be affected by the
turning of light to stone, of stone to dark and solid scope. The friend
found him continually confronted by a feathered stare. Where he worded
the interstices, the friend found him most out of it all, not always, but
sparsely attended to by himself, only a bridge recurring in a slightly
turned dream. The friend did not let the matter fall. The thing, for the
truncated friend, was that he mistook moving for still matter. The friend
broke by him, creating there a split but not amorphous grasp of a failed
gesture. The friend sought him to be immoderately constrained. The
friend saw him turning the corners proffered by those about him. He was,
if only to the friend, a man made cripple by himself, and then made like-
wise recurrently to move with performed grace. The friend made him be a
rock, and watched him worn petulant and presentably slim by the large
boulders, the frothing or sudden roughnesses. The friend knew him all
about the outside, and could see from those angles of refracted light a
small space at the center. The friend frequently made space about him, a
thing to be gendered or fondled. The friend gave, to surround him, an
aura that swept on. He became, commonly enough, a thing of lustre the
friend could and did imagine, harbored like the most uncommon of tried
objects. The friend's knuckles came up upon him. In a space of time, the
friend corrected his early knowledge, saw him an upright portrait. He
came, with too many hands of speech, suckling by the friend, leaving
him in a repeated murmur. The friend caught him in the bond of word
turning on word. He slept in a sentence the friend had made, in a welter
of sentences smoldering, in the frequented trenchant lair. The friend said
he was scrambling but in such a slow way. The friend said, once, that his
comprehension was particled and austere, that he should stop.

He walked at the ocean. To him from this came a slattering persistent
drabness. He ate diffidently. Slow pressures hallucinated around his
edges, unguarded and stiff from the wear. He wore clothing against the
slippery, the past. The days were garments, written literal, sequestering
his infrequent pulses. He cut himself twice. Frequently a small tired voice
rose from the blood. He watched the fluctuating lights at some distance
out over the black wash. Occasions rose, remittent questions with no
source or answer, sore spots in the way. He let himself eat. Further the
things of ordure were stayed. He made a long trek that took him, past
houses at night, and through an isolate clear swept day. Glistening sands

rose under his touch, bruised into time. He calculated how long it would take. Going away in a flurry of escaped grace, noisy insected trials kept him from going immediately to each spot. He spoke. The voices were things he watched. He gave himself to one position, one gesture, another, another, another. Sworn vibrations footnoted what had not yet occurred, his combined eyelid. Snorts of recognized attrition bridled by in the glance, scooping up used and reused paths of scape and escape. He wished only to be left alone in time. Even when he was least charmed by a fracturing space, he took into it. He was slowed in rushing about. His smooth shape angled off him in bits and starts of flaking noun breath. He warmed to the thought. Islands of noise were surgical to him, his scars hidden translucently under strange opaque blankets that permitted the transformations, preventing their premature arousal to no greeded end. He was part of no family, inherited or manufactured. A scope of positions were ever regardful, ever friendly, attaching his sockets to a mucuslike substance aggressive in recall. He cried twice. The worries were brothers, unbothered sisters, old in the time it takes. He watched the mixtures of surrounding peoples. Their stiff presence was resident in morose butter. He slept tight. The loose evasive reams stacked their verbiage at his pate. He cut the wood. A burning loosed its wrecked tentacles, holding him in a white curtain of moving walking, a sludge of knotted ink. He drank from himself to himself, no way else. Plural sputters of moist chaste with-drawings slew over the rest, nurturing a warm spot about the other. He was basically asleep. Already the sweatered tides were drawing, with-drawing, slaking their thirst at his limbs. He settled his young life. Grow-ing mute bonds hurtled him over the bespoken angles, allowing grasp after graft, arranging the ride. He was seventy when he was sixteen. Fig-uring it out, lorried haulings of backward works allowed themselves to him, fighting the past. He cleaned his outside reaches. The imperfected glories roosted about this, rostering in the stride of a new day. He did not stand the bickered words, from anywhere. Living closely, tied striated flicks moved him, sureing him in the eke of trivial thing on thing, glanced. He made a word do the work when he could not be quiet. A rowdy space, surnamed, did not do for him, allowing the pressure of a few laced rounds. He wondered. At the heavy traces of scarved occasion he threw scraps of his long undoing, the thing that made him seem in place, lumber and gesticulation notwithstanding. He went suredly from the quiet to the loosely distributed. He heard his mouth open and close, his eyes close. For more than a trial, all was quiet, opened by a moved brick of longing, close suddenly. He took open his clothes. The back moved around the front, the front over an exposed top, the bottom up back, side to side. He was not there. His solstice was breaking its own harvest. He was grazing in the books, triangularly. Supplicants spoke for him, each sentence a word, each word. Things came into his mind. They were out from his hand.

No lie, she knew him to be that when they met. He was rapacious in their ins and outs. They gathered their set. Their looks began slowly, knotted friends, an increase in the relaxed tide, a display of motion. They warmed in oracular trysted light that flowed from each, sure at last. The old episodes were not exactly remade. He cried again. They held to no promise spoken, to nothing, only the cold and accurate breath of some possibility which could only appear to have vanished. Their persistence was heartening, a glove proffered and shared. They made of the time, less than that and thereby something more perceptible. Resolution curtained them into a solid trope, a thing that moved and diverged, moving. He looked to recall from her a charismatic depth. The warmth made of the area a clear spectred place, landed against the struggle. Their backs fused below the breasts, their bodies tilting back through each other, so that they saw always the other's eyes, locked into a certain polished duress, a statued look of awareness made most evident in sleep. They contracted from one another, madly, eddies of feeling that swept the area clean of nothing. They carried each other about, wherever they went. They were near to each other, lonely but not alone. His elbow, raised, was level with her elbow. His raised knee touched the soft flesh above her knee. She saw him. In this way, the whole wall appeared to be her face.

RECOGNITION

Fractured bits of silence more enigmatic
and trustworthy as distances polish
verbal accumulation of sonorous power

>   where fast moves congregate
>   regularly a rush to three sources
>   of life, fear terror guilt

rubbed to reproduce frictional
moments, habits that dust and shine
fictional among clouds of trite

>   talk Moments earlier the face
>   misplaced charm, anger veered
>   from longevity as situations

of habitual looking fled
to a glance and friendship began
to relinquish its grip

>   on the distance greener
>   than white sea water and louder
>   than the heart

the arrangement of the heart
beats on the life's ideas of
fraternity and love

                              what waits among us
                  antipathy and in arrears of choices
                          made for hard regret

sidelong out of reach waiting
to reenter the opened mouth
aquatic and maternal

                              this dissolute anger
                        admits that it has scorched
                        a trial in the heart, a way

to mark recall for destruction
to make original the old lie
beating its fingers

                          into our ears and mouth
                        blocking solutions of rhythm
                              that might pound

and magnify So what
says the listener So what says
the man talking so silence

                        participates in the dissipation
                        of articulate duress, responses
                              that shutter and click

I quake to think of you
as part of myself more
admissible than grief

                          the hunter walking prisons
                        in search of a meal, anything
                              brighter than change

or trigonometry, the error
in your favor that preaches
its sermon garbled

                              and inhumane
                         a name more blatant than
                      beautiful, charged by desertion

disinterest The doldrums
are islands in that heart
sensate and mixed up

                              flashing into my eyes
                         as the head lifts holds, drops
                         we lose this vision the sight

of things mysterious and regular
split to generate reproach
and a singular

                              tribute to analysis
                         the last where this separates
                         productive of as much noise

and daring as interest
as much laughter gotten
illegibly from the start

                              a novice in any field
                         that breaks before his death
                              leaving him hard

put to recall vocations
as usually undertaken now
as inchoate and stiff

                         whole opinions are stripped
                              to stagger in waste
                              of imagined reunion

relaxed into after inadequate
pathos, partial apprehension
of greater happiness than this

                         token of wager Well I remember
                              the past now, parts of it
                              that irritate the mind, hit

upon as resting a distribution
for future consummation of targets
we never hit, the moment

                    articulate about eternity
                    but not the cracked bit
                    that sticks to hands

irregular investigation
halts, goes forward who
holds to it

                    thrust into misadventure
                    and musings that construct
                    the large obstruction

getting past more painful
than possible as easier
relinquished or retold

                    getting by this day
                    as quickly as sensation
                    admits of professed

position, here in duty
til the old ideas of self
drop and cling

                    to refuse
                    the ambivalent choice of this
                    structure, obsessive

as regret and recognition
when noticing or noticed
among faces

                    that skip by lost
                    to everything even the heat
                    that freezes the body

dripping from passion
or passionate thought encounter
of that other life

                    that follows with no weapon
                    in its empty hand but a smile
                    sliding from its face

Perhaps more arbitrary
than singular this pen
ultimate feeling

                              breaks its repetition
                    only once the time of my
                              life, the bait

that draws to no conclusion
only the past as greater speed
whipping past me

                         a discussion of violent
                         hopes retold left again
                              to the victims

the voice of affirmative slaughter
slaughtered in my throat, left
to create obstruction

                         articulate but fumbling error
                    in the book, the movement over
                    moment that speaks its distance

if not direction
its desire to get there
while mobility counts

                         for more than tolerable
                         sustenance hoped for
                         misology as the one way

out of interest or use
murmurings that glut the heart
until the misguided adventure

                         admits its irregularities
                         and relinquishes the pieces
                         of my life taken for meaning

but thrown out and off
getting rid of hatred my
love for the horizon

           now an enigma where I
          get up to speak the words
        flattened for use by the past

that rolled over crushing
resolve as will, constructing
the portions as disparate

          to recombine for pleasure
            if that The acrobatics
            of all feelings flutter

and cough up last words
to take the mind home
through recollection

            the arbitrary division
        of events, the large situation
            alone in its devotion

to itself except we
join on and are carried
or thrown against

           and shot The crucial
        crumbles again drops down
           coining new flattery

for the old adoration
of material, the substance
of devotion or despair

          an heiratic gift of vision
        pushing the heart to dogged
         apparitions, the vertigo

less insular and clear more
taken to its own understanding
of mystery and tribulation

elated that the gifted rush
of energy propels the tongue
whole dissemination of acts

that stagger to bear
the weight of individual slander
and possible misadventure

between scraped possibilities
scrapped now as the worthless anomaly
breaks the stretched arms

the breath falters another
loose bit is gone out
where it's taken

looked to for control even
less than total participation
or uneven consideration

of the continuous slopes
relaxing toward the sea
where the voice catches

and stays in, where my voice
is ignored as anger or intemperate
regret resilient and buoyant

or hoping to be but losing
pitching into descent dropping
its minuscule pitchers of sound

meaning some new token
taken for value but ignored
at last stolen

by insistent enlargement
of vocables solid and interior
congealed floating to test

the indispensable problem
of age worn against lopsided
distribution of hope

none here where the eye
sees its own hideous way
into the eye

                    the luckless happenstance
                         robbed of meaning
              sound unimaginable except for

violence flinging its hands
at the articulate lie
the redispersal of information

                    that gets us again to maintain
                    the solidity of feeling and thought
                    against what continuously assaults

and equally draws away
organizing again a pact of communion
with the bodies' liquid triggers

                         hitting the high target
                         and holding for ransom
                         the regards of a stranger

who claims indulgence or attention
before release rigged for explosion
and expansion to lost lands

                    that harbor the mysteries of growth
                    claiming to hold unheard of distances
                         and unsolved situations

seeking through my life
The details combine again to mean
how far you have come lost

                    so much unaware of varied
                    noises tapping behind the heart
                         that start up and go off

reveried and austere
more blatant less discrete
now the secrets are out

                    the old situations obtain no
                    one thing nor several but go
                    again to look for resolve

and reverberation or clandestine
tears unadmitted that fall
to the past dispensation

                    of event without watering
                    growth or flourishing needless
                    condescension to pain

or the conception of love
unwrought from actual life
the events that articulate

                    only their silence now even they
                    forgotten or told to go
                    from extravagant persuasion

to nothing less grand just
the facts of sleep and dreaming
and waking, held open

                    by the reappearance of angles
                    that need explaining need the
                    carrying away of time

spent by the tactless sea
where we wager lives as motion
hold to attentive times

                    blocking the liberty of chance
                    and swallow again the soft ways
                    of death, broken backs

staggering another step
faltering when turned answers
ignore questions for destinations

                    less palpable more where
                    lost again they go on, after
                    sturdy repose crying

in bitter and wasted talk
fugitive before the red tongue
can hold to it

                              wet the dried life
                    carry it back a place we've
                    been under investigation

but without reply
the blind tongue sweating
its syllables from the heart

                    words broke from the mind and plunged
                              into new acquaintances a few
                         quick to say what's plundered

never why this thing mattered
or that, did not the crowds
trace resistance into friends

                         who could only nod and try
                    infrequent entanglement of hope
                              taken from caked nerves

long accents of despair
caring to speak of locations
as valuable prior to loss

                              smug little whisperings
                    about reincarnation of people
                    before my eyes Hope now in

abeyance to less manageable
clarities the consequent risk
from talk, the old hammer

                              of sawdust bolting through
                    my idea of the night my way
                    of hurrying the stalled time

no friend more useful
than time we had, passed full
of each other opened

by the bitter and sad teeth
of relaxation the lethargy that
bites into my day takes

me by the hand and leads
me out of my body, reminds
me how you are taken

the words rippling sounds
that float off the head down
dark roads infrequently taken

due to memory the length
of blackness brighter
than dumb colors the greys

cramped about my head
the one time admission of happy
discharge of tension apprehended

and pushed up to hold
me there, the thick hands
that hold for no release

choice examples of disfranchised
relations that obtain no stone
from the water of betrayed time

spent in anger and annoyance
as again to take good times
and turn them

to regarded and slaughtered
unturned to fall to slow decay
the gradual falling off

of one particle the next
as suddenly gone as noticed
seen as taken down

shifting from the dark spot
of harvested time to recurrence
but not regeneration

only slow accumulation
for growth where addition
has lost to dissatisfaction

               more treaties to hapless participation
               with peoples unknown though seen
               to be there, recognized and known

perhaps, perhaps not
only music now and sweet
poetry holding the ear

               to sturdy contemplation
               of what's missed
               a tune that used to round

into afternoons but now
is not apparent though sounds
still obtain what satisfaction

               I lay down tolerable as quick
               time I gave you or others
               an immersion of conception

the self seen to ground
in all weathers to stay in
when impertinent laughter

               obtains the ear's time
               where memory night harbor
               loses the few ships

floating from adoration to recompense
the quick verbal fact, children treated
to age and disappearance

               a convoluted and long sentence
               without reprieve or reparation
               only inarticulate stance

that pushes fervor past
fever into condolenced pity
after facts of loneliness

                              the mouth turning
                         under the arbitrary hand
                       flexing inarticulate muscles

tearing words from my tongue
swollen at the sight of fear
sending its maggots in the heart

                         hardening the life firming up
                         this sloppy ear, ecstacy over
                                  the forgetting face

a history or tradition
of lives spoken for as my own
involvement with specific greeds

                         and owning nothing of defence
                           against frantic attack of fear
                                frequent and sudden here

where biographies lie down
self interest pummeling hearts
to speak again

                              of farcical and trite things
                         we hang the life to danger and
                             imagination twinned stones

to crack feet stumbling
toward participation of sad
musings and the life stoned

                              into the opened afternoon
                             evening flung out waiting
                               on the repeated question

of sleep or dreaming
the interest of new writing
pushing the mind along occasioned

                         paths where a pathetic tongue
                           leaves its mark from now on
                            import of impassioned sighs

walking the tired bones
awake and listening to full
purposed thought or musing

                    that lights in thin mind
                    making music noticeable
                    in repeated drafts of wind

forced from my teeth
Is this the place of the hearth
this life broken and ribbed

                    by repeated forages of grief
                    no magnificent past the leaf
                    turned out of sunlight to disease

and aberrant structures of loss
caked over fumbling attempts to grasp
solitude and regain this

                    verbiage of the foiled life
                    a collaboration of seasoned disintegration
                    as the father taught his son

to apparent attention
the inimitable and pacific tune
deport of eye among event

                    the habit of adoration
                    for what's done within completion
                    of one man's time the drilled

repetition the ear hearing
to give again before the eyes
and tongue, the hand holds

                    its history down for inspection
                    and incarnation as habitual
                    as other use for time and regard

of splendid disorientation
toward the diaried leisure
of time again

                    spent through broken bonds
                    and the old uses for time
                    in talk through more hours

that can't be wasted
or left to disregard
impossible abstinence

                    from my mouth's use
                    a forgoing of separation this
                    situation struggling with

the body of willed incantation
the meriter asking
recompense for laboring

                    his particular fields
                    with personal decoration
                    for unasked attention

the fictioned parts held above
for inspection this release
of blood for possible regard

                    in public the sparked talk
                    that dropped whisperings back
                    where indigenous frequency

pushed experience toward regret
of things held to or lost out
the mastication of work

                    to work it in to closed
                    hereditary systems of exchange
                    word given or took back

to be witheld, a silence
talkable and opulent in retreat
from too frequent forthright

                    indignation the low noise
                    of the stomach always at use
                    digesting specific facts

soiled in my charged life
solicited from among heads
as likely of sadness

                              the visceral minutes
                    producing conglomerate elements
                         stacked and divided farce

for greatest effort of vision
seen and forgotten the mind
halving scathed reminders

                    scattered in hasty accumulation
                    back of head where heard or seen
                              to lighten dark spells

and lightening over dark curses
the curvature of trained longing
straining to release attention

                         the profligate and indigenous
                         study of cures for the head
                         and the scorched tongue

my burnt hand holds to
Hours drill their carved armature
further depending on shores

                         we do not reach for waves
                    iridescent and seductive mauve
                    trapping an ensconced secret

the unregenerative future
pristine and sticky present where
masses the opaque trepidation

                         rumors of falling zones
                    where life builds to explode
                         tricking the onlooker

regarding extension of betrayed
moments cased in the last
days hastening

            to perfection, where perfection
                 is only obligation and regret
           the forgotten syllable for change

eradicated and stiff
shoved from sure knowledge
by other minds, intervening to hold

                and marked for interrogation
             which future minutes will obtain
                   under specified agitation

in packets of leisured time
thrown to reunion ornamented
by detail now obliterated

             so completely through contrived
           uses for my days, way spent in talk
                  and writing this down

the rites of obliteration
asking in unaltered time
a question addicted by cursive

              dedication to requarried years
                mind the final abdication
           of reason when unilateral tokens

of featured mind charging
feeling floating in aquatic scapes
accumulated and aggressive

             an emotional equivalent of life
           tried in accomodation harassed
                 and later inspired

News tonight of phases
of my past the dreams
of propriety and guilt

             ordered of intrigue and habit
          the untransmitted metric of hope
            held for later operation in

logic and equation
whatever can be seen neglected
in current combinations of sound

                    proved to be the good day
                    misapplied to recurrents
                    viewed but not focused

on for any time
here largest distractions
cored from the still heart

                    attentive to paralytic thought
                    bouncing the frayed bits
                    of broken longing traded

around uncured reflections
sadly attended and released
but attendant still

                    reading through minds
                    flashing to uncover pain
                    where it reworks my stance

against phonetic course
the slight mangling of days
worshiping applauded ways

                    of articulate interest faiths for
                    few purveyors of the choice word
                    dazzling the cut eye

intrudes as strangers
making the home dynamite
for the heart to carry

                    appareled against foul signs
                    tortured reluctance to annihilate
                    the facts of grace

spelled by worshipers alone
where inundations of sound
soil the waste presence

the sidewards approach of awards
tricked to resemble absence
of trained foresight and ample

association with unfrequented
islands of old life regulated
and torn through touch

whether soft or sudden
trails traveled produce sensation
of action and fast travel

a way seared behind the eyes
open now by my gradual recourse
to making time in pieces

long to hold harbored and made
resolute by slow distillation
stacked as the head's bulk

burden of participate trials
unordained in wailed talk
heart open and pumping

mind with dangerous flicks
of the unremitting wrist
implying involvement

dutifully to maintain
argument against falling
from resilience to remains

of life tokened by strange
depths unspoken but cried to
when time permits acclaim

for what's spoken hounded or locked
for further imagination
handling the blunt news

plummeted by pained knowledge
the posterior inundation of looking
that darkens the big dates

fomenting from the mind's
curse largely exhilarate though sparse
cares carry my day on

                              from particular message to regret
                              the furtive qualities of secrets
                              marking the last text

for slaughter in disuse
or over qualified expanse
of regard, flattened

                              and left to other eyes
                              the tardy resonance of words
                              recalling old days

pastured and unharried
by natural recourse to pain
added in life's tongue

                              to build apparent decay
                              later for lax attendance
                              upon garrulous quarrels

with a memory of events
taken down barbed by passion
retold as explication

                              proceeds from year to day
                              particular graspings after laws
                              unattended by actual peace

or respite of attack
only plodding of guarded luck
occasioning a moment

                              less multiplied by fear
                              substance prior to debate
                              or agitation the sad glance

blooming through the mind
to control respect and sounds
taking time to service recalled

                              abstractions of minute portion
                              each thing singular and tasty
                              drowning heart's urge

for compassionate surcease
or generosity of great scope
preceding the long drop

                              through aquatic times
                              by rolling of splendid seas
                              over the heart's wrecked toys

clustered or cared for
irrespective of special use
what's fractured

                              and my talk of triumphs
                              clots the throat falling back
                              once, again accumulated facts

too much before present regard
and disappearance of speculated
talk language used now

                              lost or forgotten to say
                              the words forged to alter
                              some idea of nonexistent ways

backed into the life
sore and contrary spite
clipping the dry heart

                              to sew careless moments
                              onto the heaving argument
                              leaving the last stockade

excesses of culled translucence
masquerading for lost moments
of imparted acceptance

                              tried in events
                              armed against fastidious recall
                              breaking the sliced presence

that clarifies young trials
to my attentive effort
moving back to crumbled points

                still invoking certain gratitude
           among articled and patient tenacity
             forced to regard loss and fancy

kicking what remains of patience
before asking clarification in surety
unaskable except by chance

                  whose magic ignores music
             but acceptable when occasional
            structure admits fissured entry

confluence of impartial sense
restored in variegated measure
and abhorred then

                struck in loose congregations
        filtered by currents of recent nonsense
               carrying into my thin life

mastered and sold
to obtain hasty regards
and lowered to few words

                startled under bright glazed
          eyes marking saturated and abhorred
             silences of dreamed surrender

baked in repetition of angled
assault under coated moments
meaning the arbitrary man

                so taken Moving grim arms
         avoid somnolent quarries of statement
             in frequent and ethereal harbors

labored toward in slick chains
orate and magnetic distances
of tabled griefs slaved

                                    scarred material of apt terror
                                 waking to sleepwalk dark streets
                                    where loose hands don't turn

for posterity or patience
reported associated by mirth
and gaiety stored to restore

                                          immaterial late grounds
                                    amplified to avoid insouciance
                               or too careful slaughter for surrender

that mitigates slight change
tampered in activated slop
assaulting old lands

                                       from height of maturation
                                 assured in grand attest to times
                                     trumped to present fiction

my own words slim return
into this glorified mouth
closing over sadness

                                       again posted and moored on
                                    in hopes of untoward worth
                                     flicked to gross retribution

weakness of translucent guards
facets of professed daylights
clogging the obese night

                                        spilled from my pert assent
                                   assuaging grimaced molted in facts
                                     clicking to track spoilt events

tinctured for trumpeted colleagues
inspiring habituation through response
gleaned morbid loneliness

                                       spotted for tuned resonance
                                    resembling the slayed stance
                                        of my bloodied alliance

gloated in ensconced language
applauded and singled schizoid
or mirrored annihilation

                unbridled circulation in time
            stuttering for obstinacy and lame
                  congratulations to slow

my efforts in town
slag grabbing the fast eye
held for compilation

                building to be slugged home
            largely from barbed initiation
                in payment for vague crop

junking the rotted hype
marginal by my guess of slopes
tracing remembered tomes

                in the slumped mind
            gravitated by young positions
                imitating the ancient hands

laying worlds down
for restored and edible names
coagulated in read time

                marked and quickened
            handled from garbling the lance
                freaking the tuned ears

loaded to corrugate loss
maintain intransient hoards
of sloppiest intent

                tranced retributions subliminal
            beneath chaotic soft flutterings
                of mind water below waste

frothing to tumbled access
morose content from blown
struggling to obtain land

                              furtive to tune among
                      separate ambivalence of strength
                        quickening below spilt hopes

smart angularity of movement
cursing trundled quicknesses of hate
spilling the sleek way

                            translating my slurred heart
                            in delay posterior marking
                               fragmentation of passing

unguaranteed mornings
loosed in sweet tide from talks
surmounted in traces

                                cling moribund silence
                            shake off to capitalize times
                            hoped to add congregation

smelt slung trickeries
sing insistence of sizeable traps
to commemorate long days

                            supping liquid elongation
                            recollections surfacing again
                            wrecking sweetened breathing

importance of clogged lungs
hold back restrained cadence
to foment unequatable moments

                              carving the lucid steps
                         attaining prime memory of filth
                            forming my young mind

startling inundation of fakery
mirking the slow waters flooding
toward gratifying cement

                            marking my life in rote tunes
                         detested as sung translucence
                         wasted within bound persons

bodying the heart's reasons
given to train understandable
the long floating afternoon

                reconnaissance for future omission
                overlaid by hopeful systems laid
                away from grown disappointment

stacking numbers of situations
combine as callings go out to change
unpacific logic of tribulation

                beating for massive recognition
                of timid events taken to treatment
                under articulate strain

poverty of upstanding triggers
cloaking the mind in danger
regarded for spun courage

                to beckon laziest days
                bombardment of scarce turmoil
                enough to hold current

continuous eventuality
stuffing the known contours
to crowd lost corners

                inflicting only continuous
                to crop slowed recall only there
                startled from sleep accusations

chilling flamed coinage
of brief insistence courage
may outswell captivity

                not amphibious to change
                through new heritage boggles
                eyes spelt from silence

conflict to sluice marriages
turning to encounter expectation
dragging for dim spelling

of tardy capitulation to fixtures
gassed in my tinctured place
glossed from attention

calling to create counsel
moistened in hoisting bits
from spot to spot

placing enlarged abstraction
to collect personage to net
what's not obtained

perfidy procreate and slack
under densest configuration of sounds
managing distinct preparation

tuned to condolenced sentries
guarding mouth slipshod harvest
awakens to trim adroit hearts

cluttered in verbose haste
mannered by timed laughter
obstructs congruent faces

fluctuant mimes gathered regrets
stumbling by bleak preparations
for assuaged contraries

unheralded to direct resolution
or fasten slack tributes to taste
furthered transigence spirit

might surly tainted strength
warred to acclaim mitigation
when mouths drop to restrain

tendencies between hesitations
Lopped to mark passages
seen wasting by time

studied for indigent success
sensible for standard reductions
quitted to tone slow bets

scurries for part knowing
how subtlety scourges the hands
blanketing tired lips

      sucking for more courage
     from morose strands of debt
    strewn clouds for tried sustenance

oracular briefings toward slight menace
asked far over quiet heads attending
only drillings to the dark center

      lightening the frown clutch
     from fanned tenderness to my place
    wiping struck tunes to dread ears

convalescent trillings to slight bounds
marvel to equate substantial trundlers
bleeping night air surly loss

      frocked slaughterless mornings
     few to attend quizzical investigations
    to tame slop tears from marked time

floats curled to thrust musing
clicking and beating in torn stacks
burning into mind's luck

      none to harbor stocked times
     frozen dim acquiescence to means
    tolling infrequent sound my words

breaking dim harvest of sounds
accumulate in recognized maturation
to surrend slim rebounds

      flatulent glistening morbidness
     hesitancies surrounded in fraternity
    but sloughed off reckonings stick

to attend furtive gestures thrown
ideas slowed in frail gleanings
marked in amplified nuisances

                    sluicing the jets of seen space
               hoping the nothing turns fragile down
                  spiced contributions in grasp held

to fear terror slipping stones
through mind indigenous boxing
toward masterful locking

                         holds back stopped to drown
                    fixed in anterior sounds pushed on
                      from announced participations

whetted to recognize regretted bonds
holding flicked towards stubbed passage
on fornicating events of my tunes

                    somersaulted in exasperation standings
                      sloping from memory into realization
                        slowing flicking mind's running

spurting slow over minced turns
robbed of articulation mowing waves
to whittle expectation

                         glaring to tone ears staying to tend
                       by awkward moving from now back
                         stands frozen to lock mention

tuning sleek retributive bands
to hold back sound charging in lengths
over slime immense sounds

                         ferried to accept retaliation claims
                       how maybe future holds lands no
                       quick acceptance from freak homes

tarried pick up smashed pities
grief assuaged tumultuous places
lies by bricked hands washing

                       over peaceful anticipated mind groans
                     my feared acceptance to flow gleaning
                       watered passages from life stance

marred in drab forward to stand
tried to mitigate solute feelings
but bit strength to meet regret